I AM CREATIVE

Shawn T. Letford & Genein M. Letford, M.Ed

CAFFE
STRATEGIES

For my grandma, Gwen Jefferson,
who helps me stay creative.
-STL

Illustrated by AbdullahChaudry
Additional Illustrations by Letford Media

Library of Congress Cataloging-in-Publication Data is available upon request.

ISBN 978-1-7347658-3-0

eBook ISBN 978-1-7347658-4-7

Forward

What the world needs now is IMAGINATION and CREATIVITY.

IMAGINATION is needed because a child or an adult at play is a person in wonder, curiosity, and joy. In play, our imaginal acts become the ingredients for a future VISION where new ways of being, thinking and exploring come to life.

CREATIVITY is required because it is about more than acting, singing, and the arts.

When allowed, creativity helps us discover our full human potential. We move through our fears towards a greater connection to ourselves and to one another. Specifically, creativity propels, informs, and stimulates the discovery of our unique paths to unparalleled success.

If you are an adult, ask yourself. "Have I stopped imagining, playing, and creating?"

What the world needs now is a commitment that you will inspire our young ones to expand their creative minds, so that they may soar beyond the boxes of this society to create mind-bending solutions for our future. We encourage you to join them as well.

You are creative.

-Dr. Gloria Chance
Psychologist, Creativity Expert
CEO, The Mousai Group

When I wake up each morning,
I try to start my day
by thinking: "I'm creative -
in every single way!"

I look beyond the surface
of what my eyes can see.
I listen, smell, and touch things
to know all that can be.

2

I love to ponder questions like "How'd that come to be?" or "Why?" or "What is missing?" That's curiosity!

3

When studying an object,
I view it all around.
I may climb high above it
or lie down on the ground.

I feel all my emotions
when learning something new.
And in your eyes and movements,
I see your feelings, too!

Sometimes the world feels giant,
my thinking really scatters.
But when I keep it simple,
I see what truly matters.

"Now this thing is like that thing..."
I often like to think.
I love to make connections
and see how items link.

When dancing with my daddy,
I hear them in the beats.
They're patterns, all around us,
from nature to the streets!

8

Bark acts like a protector
of every single tree.
This poet way of thinking
is called analogy!

When meeting different people
from places old and new,
I start to see what they see
and broaden my world view.

Imagination takes me
to places far away.
My brain grows even bigger
with every game I play!

When I pick up my paintbrush,
I always have a ball.
Do you sing, dance, or doodle?
The arts are for us all!

When sharing my ideas,
I try all kinds of ways,
to help all different learners
get what I'm trying to say.

When sitting with a question,
just waiting for a clue,
I look inside for signals
and know just what to do!

My brain has many circuits,
like robots but way more.
It brings my thoughts together
and helps my ideas soar!

I end the day so grateful
and go to bed with glee
when I have shared with courage
my creativity!

Parents, Teachers, and Caregivers

Here are the *16 Diamond Tools of Creative Thinking* that Shawn experiences throughout the book. Even though children harbor these creative abilities innately, you can still strengthen these skills within them and redevelop them within yourself. Here's how:

◆ 1- 'I Believe' (Foundational Beliefs Systems)
Do you believe they are creative? The first step to improving creative thinking is to understand what creativity is, know how to develop it and believe THEY ARE CREATIVE! So are you!

◆ 2- Paying Attention Pays Off (Sensory Observation)
Creative thinking arises from knowledge. Through observation of the senses (sight, sound, taste, touch, smell) and cognition, they are able to increase the amount of data available for creative thinking. Strengthen their senses and multisensory experiences for more connections within their brains and across subjects.

◆ 3- Return to the 'Wonder Years' (Curiosity)
Children arrive on Earth very curious but this vital skill for creative thinking lowers with familiarity and routine. Improve their desire see beyond convention. Learn how to ask better questions and discover how the most awe inspiring ideas come from the most mundane of objects.

◆ 4- Framing the Birds, Bears and Bugs! (Perspective Shifting/ Reframing)
When they shift various perspectives of an experience, viewpoint, or event, it reveals new associations and insights about previously unchallenged concepts. Allow them to role play the perspective they are trying to understand.

5- <u>All the Feels</u> (Emotional Intelligence/Empathy)
Learning how to feel the emotional information of a situation exposes new insight. Use discussion and interactive activities to improve their ability to process, communicate and express emotional information.

6- <u>A Creative 'KISS': Keep It Simple Silly!</u> (Abstracting)
Keep It Simple Silly! Remove excess information to get to the pure nature of something (an object, concept or problem). This creative tool allows them to extract the critical essence of their ideas.

7- <u>Let's Connect 4</u> (Making Connections)
Everything is connected to everything. Finding those connections bridges unlike items together and reveals critical elements that would otherwise go unnoticed.

8- <u>Purposeful Patterns</u> (Pattern Recognition and Pattern Forming)
Being sensitive to pattern discovery and pattern creation is the key to innovation. Pattern recognition is dependent upon observation. Trends and innovative discoveries are best identified through observing patterns.

9- <u>The Function of Metaphorical Messages</u> (Metaphors/Analogies)
Metaphorical training helps them see relationships on a variety of levels. Creative development that includes metaphorical and analogy development will improve the awareness of functional relationships between objects and concepts for innovative ideas to surface.

10- <u>Diverse Demos</u> (Diversity of Thought/People/Experiences)
Exposing children to various cultures, arts and experiences exposes unseen revelations about the systems (social, educational, political, professional systems) in which they are in. External travel causes internal reflection and insight.

◆ 11- <u>Play On!</u> (Play/Imagination)
Let us play! When people experiment in play without the fear of consequence, they are able to test, hypothesize, gain feedback and correct mistakes to gain a new perspective on how things work. It reveals new possibilities and transfers knowledge into real life applications. Adults need play just as much as children!

◆ 12- <u>Start With Art</u> (Multi-Modal Communication/Proprioception)
The arts give us a deeper way to feel, communicate, investigate and explore. And it's this insight that can increase creative thinking to find deeper meaning in our experiences.

◆ 13- <u>I Like To Move It, Move It!</u> (Transference/Transforming/Translation)
Transferring ideas from one medium to another pulls out hidden elements while strengthening their ability to communicate ideas clearly and concisely. Creative children can create in one mode, define the problem in another mode, and then solve it and express it through another mediums.

◆ 14- <u>Divine Downloads</u> (Intuition/6th Sense/8th Arrow)
The greatest creative thinkers are in tune with their intuition which delivers inspirational hunches. Record those 'aha' moments! EUREKA!

◆ 15- <u>Better Together</u> (Synthesizing)
Integrating the senses and knowledge to reveal 'the wholeness' of the idea or solution is the critical step to innovation. The whole is greater than its parts and developing 'whole brain' creative thinkers is key!

◆ 16- <u>Courage</u> (Conative Execution)
The confidence to push past conventional thinking, apply these Diamond Tools and share your creative ideas takes courage. Many ideas die within the creator because of fear. Build their courage to create, contribute and make an impact for their communities!

I AM CREATIVE!

Genein Letford is an award-winning educator, best-selling author and global speaker on Intercultural Creativity®. As a TEDx speaker and top creativity trainer, she has inspired many educators to be aware of their cultural lenses and creative abilities in order to produce innovative ideas for the classroom and workspace. She is the founder and Chief Creative Officer of CAFFE Strategies, LLC which trains administrators, educators and employees to unleash their Intercultural Creativity® for themselves and in their classrooms. Pulling from her fifteen years of working with creative geniuses, her unique curriculum utilizes metaphorical strategies, heightened observation techniques and the creative arts to reawaken intuitive thinking in her attendees. Genein believes creative thinking paired with cultural competency are critical 21st Century skills and she is often called 'America's Creativity Coach' for her work in reigniting Intercultural Creativity® in our youth and in our workforce. Genein lives in Arizona with her curious husband Shayne and Shawn The Creative Kid.

@GeneinLetford

Shawn 'The Creative Kid' Letford published his first book at three years old and is on a mission to help the world be more creative. When he first arrived on Earth, he was in awe of lights. Now, at three years old, the world of sprinklers is his main obsession. He loves being, thinking and sharing his creativity. Follow his creative adventures on social media!

LinkedIn: Shawn The Creative Kid
IG: @Creativekid_SL
Facebook: @CreativeKidSL
Twitter: @Creativekid_SL

Creatively Grateful

Creating this book was a creative adventure: ups and downs and all arounds! But it was more rewarding than I could have ever imagined. None of this would have been possible without the support of my family. Thank you Daddy for making the book a final masterpiece. Thanks mommy for seeing all the creative things I do throughout the day and helping me share it with the world. Thank you to my grandparents, aunts, uncles and cousins.

To my illustrator Mr. Abdullah Chaudry, thank you for taking the time to look at the funny pictures of me being creative. I had lots of facial expressions to illustrate! A big thank you to the best poem editor, Ms. Meeg Pincus. You made my rhyme step in time! Thank you Mr. Erik Seversen for reading it through as well. Thank you Ms. Monica Montoya for taking my pictures and making me smile. You're an easy person to smile for. I get to be creative with lots of toys from Lakeshore so I have to give a big thanks to Mr. Kevin Carnes for the Lakeshore spaceship and more! Thank you Dr. Chance for sticking up for our imagination! The forward you wrote was great! A big gracias goes to 'mi otra familia' that I spend time with while my mommy is working. Gracias Tia Belen, Tio Alex, Jackie and Erik for giving me creative activities to explore while Tia Belen is taking care of me. Soy Creativo!

I'm eternally grateful to those who financially supported this book on GoFundMe. This includes Grandma Gwen, Aunt Genae, Aunt Greta, Ms. Kat and Mr. Lee, Ms. Audrey, Ms. Fanny and my friend Melody, Ms. Enjoli, Ms. Jonaye, Mr. Oscar, Mr. Trey, Ms. Namuli and my friend Kabaka, Ms. Claudia, Ms. Jacqueline, Mr. Manuel, Ms. Ilene, Mr.Jose, Ms. Juana, Ms. Nancy, Ms. Amy, Ms. Jasmine, Ms. Cherry and all the anonymous angel donors that supported as well. You know who you are! Your belief in this project and financial investment in this book will go around the world while also shining bright in my heart! Stay kind and be creative!

-Shawn 'The Creative Kid'
3½ years old